JONATHAN SWIFT

T0346159

JONATHAN SWIFT

THE LESLIE STEPHEN LECTURE

DELIVERED BEFORE THE UNIVERSITY OF CAMBRIDGE
ON 26 MAY 1917

BY

CHARLES WHIBLEY, M.A.

HONORARY FELLOW OF JESUS COLLEGE, CAMBRIDGE

Cambridge :
at the University Press
1917

CAMBRIDGE
UNIVERSITY PRESS

University Printing House, Cambridge CB2 8BS, United Kingdom

Published in the United States of America by Cambridge University Press, New York

Cambridge University Press is part of the University of Cambridge.

It furthers the University's mission by disseminating knowledge in the pursuit of education, learning and research at the highest international levels of excellence.

www.cambridge.org
Information on this title: www.cambridge.org/9781107688360

© Cambridge University Press 1917

This publication is in copyright. Subject to statutory exception
and to the provisions of relevant collective licensing agreements,
no reproduction of any part may take place without the written
permission of Cambridge University Press.

First published 1917
First paperback edition 2014

A catalogue record for this publication is available from the British Library

ISBN 978-1-107-68836-0 Paperback

Cambridge University Press has no responsibility for the persistence or accuracy of
URLs for external or third-party internet websites referred to in this publication,
and does not guarantee that any content on such websites is, or will remain, accurate
or appropriate.

PREFACE

WHEN the University of Cambridge honoured me by inviting me to deliver the Leslie Stephen lecture, I thought I was in duty bound to go to the 18th century for my subject. For Leslie Stephen has made the 18th century his own by right of conquest. Nor was I deterred from choosing to speak of Jonathan Swift by the reflection, that I should take a view of him and his writings, which was not the view of Leslie Stephen, whom this lecture commemorates. If controversy be the athletics of literature, as I think it is, then Leslie Stephen was not of those who would have resented disagreement. For he was an athlete always—on the running path, on the High Alps, and in his study. Thus was I guided in the choice of my subject.

JONATHAN SWIFT

The most of writers are freed by death from the enmities and controversies of life. Of Swift alone it may be said that the evil opinion they held of him, who had felt his righteous scourge, was not interred with his bones. Ever since the light of his genius went out in the darkness of misery, he has been attacked, with a violent rancour, by critics who regarded him not as a great historical figure, but as a miscreant who had inflicted upon them a personal injury. These critics clamoured in a loud voice not for judgment, but for vengeance. The passage of a century did not mitigate their animosity nor soften their rage. For Macaulay, Swift was an apostate politician, a ribald priest, a perjured lover, a heart burning with hatred against the whole human race, a mind richly stored with images from the dunghill and the

7

lazar-house. These expletives mean nothing more than that Macaulay was a Whig, and that Swift was a Tory, a kind of antiquated Croker, whose varlet's jacket it was the proper business of an Edinburgh Reviewer to dust. Thackeray's attack upon Swift is far more virulent and less easily explained than Macaulay's. There is no vileness, of which a Yahoo might be capable, that the author of *Esmond* does not attribute to his foe. Indeed I do not know why the sinister figure, which Thackeray chooses to invent, should have been included in a gallery of English Humourists at all. There is little humour in the ruffian, whose very virtues were, according to Thackeray, vices in disguise, who insulted those whom he succoured, who flung his benefactions in poor men's faces, who was "boisterously servile," and who, a "life-long hypocrite," put his apostasy out to hire. Of Swift's *Modest Proposal* Thackeray has nothing wiser to say than that "he enters the nursery with the tread and gaiety of an ogre." Even *Gulliver*, which, defying time and place, is as fresh to-day as when it was written, and has found a home in every corner of the globe, which is read by children for its fable and by men for its satire, merely arouses the wrath of the critic: "As for the moral," says Thackeray, "I think it horrible, shameful, unmanly, blasphemous; and giant and great as this Dean is, I say we should hoot him."

Hooting is perhaps not the soundest method of criticism, and yet were Swift all that he has been painted, hooting would seem mild and inefficient. "If you had been his inferior in parts"—again it is Thackeray who speaks—"his equal in mere social station, he would have bullied, scorned, and insulted you; if, undeterred by his great reputation, you had met him like a man, he would have quailed before you, and not had the pluck to reply, and gone home, and years after written a foul epigram about you—watched for you in a sewer, and come out to assail you with a coward's blow and a dirty bludgeon." Of course this amazing invective, which has no touch with reality, is an expression of Victorian prejudice and no more.

Thackeray himself does not attempt to justify it, and it is not worth refutation. But it makes us wonder why Swift, alone of men and writers, should be thus singled out for posthumous obloquy, and persuades us to discover if we can what definite charge has been brought against his character and his genius.

He was a misanthrope, says the Friend of Man. And Swift himself gave some colour to this charge. In a famous letter to Pope he explained the system upon which he had governed himself many years. "I have ever hated all nations, professions, and communities," he says, "and all my love is towards individuals: for instance, I hate the tribe of lawyers, but I love Counsellor Such-a-One, and Judge Such-a-One....But principally I hate and detest that animal called man, although I heartily love John, Peter, Thomas, and so forth." And which, indeed, is better: to love John, Peter, and Thomas with a constant heart, or feigning a bland and general love of abstract humanity, to wreak a wild revenge upon individuals? We know well enough whither universal philanthropy leads us. The Friend of Man is seldom the friend of men. At his best, he is content with a moral maxim, and buttons up his pocket in the presence of poverty. "*I* give thee sixpence! I will see thee damned first." It is not for nothing that Canning's immortal words were put in the mouth of the Friend of Humanity, who finding that he cannot turn the Needy Knife-grinder to political account, gives him kicks for ha'pence, and goes off in "a transport of republican enthusiasm." Such is the Friend of Man at his best. At his worst, he expresses his philanthropy most eloquently upon the scaffold. Robespierre and the infamous Joseph Le Bon, for instance, loved humanity so dearly that they delighted to see the heads of men and women too fall beneath the knife of the guillotine. Perhaps they thought of Humanity as a tree, which would grow in greater strength and beauty, the more savagely it was pruned.

For this philanthropy, then, Swift cared nothing. He loved such of his friends, as he deemed worthy of his love, with an unchanging loyalty. He did not close his eyes to the general infamy of mankind. He had lived at too close quarters with politics and politicians to harbour the genial, easy-going illusions of the philanthropist. While he knew the true worth of his friends, he admitted that such men as they were rare visitants upon this earth. "Oh! if the world had but a dozen Arbuthnots in it, I would burn my Travels"—thus he wrote to Pope soon after the publishing of *Gulliver*. But there were not a dozen Arbuthnots, and the irony of *Gulliver* was abundantly justified.

And then we hear Thackeray objecting that he would not have liked to live with Swift, he would not have been a friend of the great Dean. As he lay in no danger of this awkward companionship, the objection seems irrelevant. But there is no doubt that the best of Swift's contemporaries were very eager to live with him. He was, so to say, a great centre of amiability and friendship. He held together, in pleasant bondage to himself, the most highly distinguished men of his time. Since he did not waste his affection upon the vague thing, called humanity, he had all the more to spare for those friends who loved and understood him. Even when he is as far from them as Dublin is from London, he dominates them by the mere force of his constancy. You feel that they would not have thought so warmly one of another, if they had not united in thinking warmly of him.

Nor did he take a light or trivial view of the bond which he believed should hold good men together. "I have often endeavoured," he wrote to Pope, in 1723, "to establish a friendship among all men of genius, and would fain have it done. They are seldom above three or four contemporaries, and if they could be united would drive the world before them. I think it was so among the poets in the time of Augustus, but envy, party, and pride have hindered it among us." Swift's was a dream which could never come true. What could men of genius, held together by an indissoluble bond, achieve against the settled opposition of mediocrity? They could indulge their talent for friendship—that is all. And in this indulgence assuredly Swift never fell below his opportunity. Those friends he had, and their adoption tried, he kept until the last separation of death. They belonged to many worlds, and Swift was the captain of them all. If they were busied with affairs, Swift knew how to separate the man from the politician. "I always loved you just so much the worse for your station," he wrote to Harley in the hour of Harley's trial, "for in your public capacity you have often angered me to the heart, but, as a private man, never once." His affection for Harley survived all the chances and changes of life, even the bitter feud, which separated St John from his leader; and the affection was transmitted faithfully to Harley's son.

So too Ormond, Peterborough and Bathurst delighted in his companionship, without thought of self. But the four friends, whose names will ever be linked with Swift's, are Bolingbroke and Arbuthnot, Pope and Gay. There is nothing in the correspondence, which passed between these great men, that does not do them honour. Transparently sincere himself, Swift schooled even Pope to sincerity. When Swift is in Ireland, they are urgent one and all that he should visit them in London. They disclose their literary plans to him, as to one who is always ready with counsel and never at fault. And Swift treated them, each after his kind, with the truthfulness of a friend.

Indulgent to Gay's foibles, he addresses him as a father might address a loved and careless son. He would have him save his money, that he might live happily independent of court and patronage. He is anxious always lest Gay should squander his talent unworthily, and be content to repeat himself and his old successes. And yet so nicely did he measure the limits of Gay's fancy, that it was he who suggested the theme of *The Beggar's Opera*. "What think you of a Newgate pastoral," wrote Swift to Pope, in his desire to fit Gay with a subject, "among the thieves and whores there?" And Gay repaid his friend with a joyous devotion, sent him the news of the town, touched lightly as he alone could touch it, persuaded the Duchess of Queensberry to entertain the Dean with letters, and was tireless in transmitting the kindly messages of his friends. Nor did he forget Swift in the very presence of death. "He asked for you a few hours before," wrote Pope, and Swift showed his sensibility by endorsing Pope's letter, a sad messenger of woe, with the words: "On my dear friend Mr Gay's death; received December 15th, but not read till the 20th, by an impulse foreboding some misfortune."

It mattered not which of the four Swift addressed. He wrote to him fully and faithfully what was in his mind. Now and again he seems to remember that Pope is vastly superior to him in the artistry of verse. Of this superiority he makes full confession in the poem on his own death:

> In Pope I cannot read a line,
> But with a sigh I wish it mine;
> When he can in one couplet fix
> More sense than I can do in six.

But otherwise his comradeship knows no

restraint. Not unnaturally it is with Bolingbroke that he is on terms of closest
intimacy. He had shared that great man's
secrets from the time of their first ac-
quaintance. Together they had lived
through the last troubled years of the
Queen's reign. Together they had fallen
into disgrace, and had known the misery
of exile. And thus retired, both of them,
from the competition of life, they were
free to discuss philosophy and to defy the
Whigs. While Bolingbroke affected a
contempt of the world, Swift cried *Vive
la Bagatelle*, and hoped to silence the
voice of regret. But, if Bolingbroke
was most intimate to his understanding,
Arbuthnot was nearest to Swift's heart.
The two men were of the same tempera-
ment, scholars and ironists both. Yet it
was for themselves that Swift and Arbuthnot loved one another, not for their
intellectual gifts. "All your honour,
generosity, good nature, good sense, wit,
and every other praise-worthy quality,"
wrote Swift to Arbuthnot in 1714, "will
never make me think one jot the better
of you. That time is now some years

17

past; and you will never mend in my opinion. But really, brother, you have a sort of shuffle in your gait; and now I have said the worst that your most mortal enemy could say of you with truth." And twelve years later, in complete forgetfulness, I am sure, of Swift's letter, and not in any competition with his characteristic humour, Arbuthnot echoed the compliment. "I had a great deal of discourse," said he, "with your friend, her Royal Highness. She insisted upon your wit and good conversation. I told her Royal Highness, that was not what I valued you for, but for being a sincere honest man, and speaking truth when others were afraid to speak it."

It has been said by Swift's enemies that he slunk away from his friends, and the truth is that the links of the chain which bound the five together were never weakened. Hear what Bolingbroke wrote to Swift after twenty years of companionship. "I loved you almost twenty years ago: I thought of you as well as I do now, better was beyond the power of conception, or to avoid an equivoque, beyond the extent of my ideas.... While my mind grows daily more independent of the world, and feels less need of leaning on external objects, the ideas of friendship return oftener, they busy me, they warm me more. Is it that we grow more tender as the moment of our great separation approaches? Or is it that they who are to live together in another state, for *vera amicitia non nisi inter bonos*, begin to feel that divine sympathy which is to be the great bond of their future society? There is no one thought which soothes my mind like this." These words breathe the true spirit of loyalty, and assure us that *inter bonos* both Bolingbroke and Swift must be counted. And Arbuthnot too sent from his death-bed a last message to Swift. " I am afraid, my dear friend," he wrote, " we shall never more see each other in this world. I shall, to the last moment preserve my love and esteem for you, being well assured you will never leave the paths of virtue and honour; for all that is in this world is not worth the least deviation from this way." I do not think that we shall match

elsewhere this record of noble friend-
ships, at once gay and sincere. Yet there
are those who condemn the gaiety, and
doubt the sincerity. To one distinguished
biographer a letter addressed by Bolingbroke to the three Yahoos of Twickenham, Pope, Gay, and Swift, and ending
with the benediction, "Mirth be with
you," suggests nothing happier "than the
mirth of Redgauntlet's companions, when
they sat dead (and damned) at their ghastly
revelry, and their laughter passed into
such wild sounds as made the daring
piper's 'very nails turn blue[1].'"

And Swift was not content merely to
write letters to his friends. He looked
upon practical benevolence as the first
duty of friendship. If he could not com-
mand the preferment he wished for himself, he could at least help to ensure the
preferment of others. The list of those
whom he aided in the hour of his influence is long and various. As Mr Lecky
says, "there is scarcely a man of genius

[1] It is true that this letter was written during Stella's
illness. But Bolingbroke knew nothing of this illness, and
Swift was not of those who unpack their hearts to their
friends.

of the age who was not indebted to him."
When service might be rendered, he for-
got himself and the claims of party. He
collected a thousand guineas for Pope's
Iliad. Steele and Rowe and Parnell all
owed places to his amiable pressure. He
commended Congreve to Harley, and
was able to write in a letter to Stella :
"So I have made a worthy man happy,
and that is a good day's work."

But no better example of Swift's kind-
liness can be found than his treatment of
young William Harrison, a little pretty
fellow and a Whig, who had come from
the University of Oxford a year or two before Swift encountered him. Now young
Harrison had more ambition than talent,
more hopefulness than industry. He was
witty and pleasant in company, and "the
fine fellows," said Swift, "invited him to
the tavern, and asked him to pay his shot."
Such as he was Swift was resolved to make
his fortune. He set him up in a new
Tatler, when Steele's came to an end.
He busied himself about printers and
proofs. He suggested· articles or wrote
them. He persuaded Congreve to help

the young editor, and Congreve, generous as Swift, wrote a paper for him, in spite of his blindness. Nothing was left undone that might ensure the success of the venture. One night Swift confides in Stella that he is "tired with correcting Harrison's trash," and that he is afraid that the little toad has not the vein for it. Indeed he had not, and no sooner was Swift convinced of his inaptitude than he began to seek other employment for him. Already he had made him known to St John and Harley, and through their influence obtained for him a secretary's post at the Hague; but young Harrison, doomed to misfortune, came back from Holland only to die. Swift was tireless in help until the end, and sketched the last scene in a letter to Stella. "I took Parnell this morning," he wrote, "and we walked to see poor Harrison. I had the hundred pounds in my pocket. I told Parnell I was afraid to knock at the door; my mind misgave me. I knocked, and his man told me his master was dead an hour before."

And when Swift went an exile into

Ireland, he extended his literary patronage to all the sad poets and faded bluestockings of Dublin. He corrected their poor copies of verses, he pretended to discover genius, where not a spark was shining, and he sent them off to London, with letters in their pocket to Pope and Bolingbroke and Gay. Their reception at Twickenham was not always gracious, and oftentimes the Yahoos by the Thames expostulated justly with the Dean. But Swift, commonly the sternest of judges, softened his criticism for the incompetent, and if he were pitiless to the pretentious impostor, he had ever a word of over-kind sympathy for the modest aspirant.

Thus the charge that Swift was a misanthrope, if we interpret the term rightly, has, I think, no support in fact. The other charge of cynicism, which has oftentimes been brought against him, is equally insecure. Now the cynic may be defined as one who looks upon life and morals with an indifferent curiosity, whose levity persuades him to smile upon the vices of others, and to let them go to destruction each his own way. Of this

kind of cynicism Swift was wholly innocent. He may be absolved also of that
cynicism, which the dictionary defines as
"captious fault-finding." The heart that
was torn by *saeva indignatio*, to use a phrase
from the epitaph he composed for himself, was no cynic's heart. The truth is
that he was a born idealist, with no desire
either to snarl or to smile at life. The
master-passion of his mind was anger
against injustice and oppression. To the
articles of his own faith he was always
loyal. The profitable changes of the
renegade were as far beyond his reach as
the wiles of the time-server. That he
thought himself ill-used by the world,
that he knew his preferment was incom-
mensurate with his worth and talent is
evident. But he would rather have spoken
out what was in his mind than have won
the mitre of an archbishop.

Throughout a long career he wrote
nothing that did not clamour for expression, and no consideration of prudence
ever hindered him from doing what he believed his duty. I will choose one incident
out of many to illustrate my meaning.

The Duke of Schomberg was killed at the Battle of the Boyne, and was buried in St Patrick's Cathedral. When Swift was appointed dean, no stone marked the soldier's resting-place, and Swift, to whom nothing was indifferent, which touched the beauty and dignity of the Church committed to his charge, demanded of Schomberg's heirs, by letters and by the intervention of friends, that they should put up a suitable monument. The demand was made in vain, and Swift punished the neglect and discourtesy by erecting a monument himself, and by commemorating in a lapidary inscription the careless ingratitude of Schomberg's descendants. Had Swift wished to stand well with the Court, he would not thus have risked its good opinion. George II declared in a fury that Dr Swift's design was to make him quarrel with the King of Prussia, and henceforth regarded the Dean of St Patrick's with a still acuter suspicion. But Swift had done what he thought right, and made to Lord Bathurst a characteristic and ironical comment upon his own action. "Thus I endeavour," said he, "to do justice to my station, and give no offence."

But it was in his Irish policy that Swift proved most clearly the pure and lofty idealism that burned within him. In defending the Irish from oppression he was not swayed by the motives of patriotism; he did not yield even to a personal prejudice. He was not an Irishman. No drop of Irish blood flowed in his veins. As he said himself, he was born in Ireland by a mere accident, and he bitterly resented the superstition that the children of a man, living in Ireland, are all Irish, "while a thief transported to Jamaica, and married to a battered Drury Lane hackney jade, should produce true Britons." Nor did he love Ireland. He knew himself condemned to die there as he said "like a poisoned rat in a hole," and gladly would he have found an excuse to live out his life among his friends in England. But he hated injustice and dishonour, wherever he saw them, and so he became as wise and valiant a champion of Ireland as that unhappy country ever found.

With characteristic frankness he disclaimed the name of patriot. "I do profess without affectation," he wrote to Pope, "that your kind opinion of me as a patriot, since you will call it so, is what I do not deserve; because what I do is owing to perfect rage and resentment, and the mortifying sight of slavery, folly, and baseness about me, among which I am forced to live." He was furiously enraged against the Irish for not making the best of their resources, against the English for the unjust restrictions which they put upon Irish industries. It irked him that all the profitable offices in the country should be held by those to whom reversions had been granted, that the notorious Bubb Dodington, for instance, should be Clerk of the Pells, at a salary of £2500 a year. And when once he had been convinced of the prevailing injustice, he put all the eloquence of his scorn at the service of Ireland. First came his proposal for the universal use of Irish manufactures, utterly rejecting and renouncing everything wearable that was made in England. He was in favour of total exclusion. " I should rejoice to see an English stay-lace thought scandalous," he said, "and become a topic for censure at visits and tea-tables." He applied the fable of Pallas and Arachne to England and Ireland, and thought England harsher than the goddess. He spoke in vain to a people, indifferent to prosperity, a people which would rather have kept in the fashion, by wearing foreign stuffs and silks, than have ensured the success of Irish manufactures.

But it was the patent granted to William Wood, a gentleman eminent in the hardware trade, to impose a new copper coinage upon Ireland, which stirred the savage indignation of Swift to its depths. That there was a great lack of pence and ha'pence in Ireland is certain. The want was not supplied most economically by promising comfortable bribes to many personages about the Court, and by making the egregious Wood a present of £3000 a year for eight years. In all these transactions the need and benefit of Ireland were forgotten, and Swift made it his business to paint in the darkest colours what he deemed an injustice done to a whole country. *The Drapier's Letters*, which were sold by the Flying Stationers for two pence in the streets of Dublin, had their due effect. They forced the government to withdraw Wood's ha'-pence, and they set Swift, who, in Pope's phrase, had unbound "Ireland's copper chains," upon the topmost pinnacle of glory.

Henceforth he was the idol of the Irish people. Once when he returned from London to Dublin, bonfires were lit in his honour, and peals of bells rang out their welcome. In vain did Walpole and the Whigs clamour for his arrest. They were asked if they had 10,000 men to spare, for assuredly the Dean could not be taken with less. The utmost that Swift's enemies dared to do was to throw the printer into jail, though the secret of authorship was so ill kept that the whole of Dublin knew that it was Swift's hand and none other that had written *The Drapier's Letters*. A verse which was sent broadcast over the town, and which was at once a confession and a threat, made all doubt impossible: "And the people said unto Saul, Shall Jonathan die, who hath wrought this great salvation in Israel? God forbid: as the Lord liveth, there shall not one hair of his head fall to the ground; for he hath wrought with God this day. So the people rescued Jonathan, that he died not."

And the same eyes of idealism, with which he looked on Ireland, Swift turned upon the larger world of morals in *Gulliver's Travels*. The sentimentalists have condemned the conclusions of this celebrated satire as hateful and blasphemous, and it is not easy to follow their argument. If they pretend that it is the purpose of the famous fourth voyage to preach the superiority of all horses to all men, they have singularly misread the fable. Nor is Swift, when he makes the King of Brobdingnag a scourge, wherewith to beat the politicians and plotters of his own land, passing a universal sentence upon the human race. Gulliver himself is not represented as the only man who has escaped the vices of his country.

And the King makes no more than a general comment upon the intrigues of politicians, when he says that, by the answers he has "wringed and extorted" from Gulliver, he cannot but conclude "the bulk of your natives to be the most pernicious race of little odious vermin, that nature ever suffered to crawl upon the surface of the earth." What more do we find here than a picturesque interpretation of Walpole and his government?

It is plain, moreover, that Swift puts in the mouth of the Brobdingnagian King his own hopes and opinions. By a stroke of irony, he confesses that the learning most highly prized by the giants, being wholly applied to the improvement of agriculture and the mechanical arts, would be as little esteemed among us, as the ideas, entities, abstractions and transcendentals, which we ourselves prized, would be esteemed among them. It is plain also that Swift accepts as his own the generous creed of the King of Brobdingnag, "that whoever could make two ears of corn, or two blades of grass, to grow upon a spot of ground where only one grew before, would deserve better of mankind, and do more essential service to his country, than the whole race of politicians put together." Two hundred years after Swift we have re-discovered the truth of this simple doctrine, and nothing but a vain superstition of party can dismiss the moral of Gulliver as shameful, horrible, blasphemous.

Why, then, should Swift have been thus monstrously misunderstood? Why should he still be pursued after death, by a kind of personal venom? I think for the very reason that he was no cynic. He could not regard leniently the folly of those about him. He did not write for his own pleasure, or to put money in his pocket. He wrote in scorn of stupidity, or with a fixed desire to reform abuses. He does not temper the wind of his wrath to his shorn victims. He does not bring an easy message of perfectibility to a sanguine world. He is even cruel in his denunciation of abuses, and those who regard literature as an anodyne do not like cruelty. But let it be remembered that Swift's cruelty was always justified.

Secondly Swift was a great master of irony—the greatest that ever was born in these isles. Great enough to teach a lesson to Voltaire himself, and to inspire the author of *Jonathan Wild*. And irony does not make for popularity. The plain man likes a plain statement, and resents it, if his idle brain be confused. Swift was frankly conscious of his gift:

> Arbuthnot is no more my friend,
> Who dares to irony pretend,
> Which I was born to introduce,
> Refin'd it first, and shew'd its use.

Thus he wrote with perfect truth. He was born to introduce irony, but he did not succeed in making it understood. Now irony has been described as the boomerang of literature, and assuredly it comes back upon the head of the hero who dares to wield it. Though we all know what it is when we see it, a definition is not easy. The wise author of *The Courtier* thus describes it: "There is in like manner an honest and comely

33

kind of jesting that consisteth in a certain dissimulation, when a man speaketh one thing and privily meaneth another. I speak not of the manner that is clean contrary, as if one should call a dwarf a giant, and a black man white, or one most ill-favoured beautiful, because they be open contraries. But when with a grave and dry speech and in sporting a man speaketh pleasantly that he hath not in his mind."

Such a dissimulation, indeed, covers all the kinds of irony—the Sophoclean irony, in accord with which a secret, known to the audience, eludes the personages on the Stage; the Socratic irony, which is no more than a pretended lack of knowledge ; and the irony of Swift, in which the word and the spirit are opposed to the sense, and in which a heightened effect is produced by overstating the other side of the case. There is no artifice of literature more instantly effective for those who appreciate it. There is none more fertile in misunderstanding. In England especially it is used at the writer's peril. That wonderful

masterpiece, *Jonathan Wild*, is still condemned as an affront upon sound morality.
George Meredith was asked to wait
twenty years for readers, because he could
not resist an ironic presentation. But it
is Swift who has suffered most bitterly for
the irony which was in his blood. All
the sins and vices which he castigated
have been visited by the unwary upon
his innocent head. When he wrote in *Mr
Collins's Discourse*, that "the Clergy who
are so impudent to teach the people the
doctrines of faith, are all either cunning
knaves or mad fools," his enemies cried
out upon him for an atheist. When in
a second tract he declared that another
" advantage proposed by the abolishing
of Christianity, is the clear gain of one
day in seven, which is now entirely lost,
and consequently the kingdom one-
seventh less considerable in trade, business and pleasure," he was denounced as
a blasphemous hypocrite, who had gone
into the Church with the base hope of
gain. When, with his heart full of rage
at the misery of Dublin, he wrote his
Modest Proposal, he was charged with an

unnatural hankering after human flesh.
And this obstinate refusal to understand
the meaning and purpose of irony has
turned *A Tale of a Tub*, that amazing
riot of wit and satire, into a work of dan-
gerous example. Yet Swift could no
more avoid irony than Rabelais could
avoid ridicule. It was an integral part
of his temper and his genius. Thus and
thus only could he express the truth
that was in him, and so fine an instrument did irony become in his skilful hands,
that none has ever used it since with a
like mastery and to the same effect.

It has been the custom to compare
Swift with Rabelais. We all remember
Pope's amiable criticism:

Whether he choose Cervantes' serious air,
Or laugh and shake in Rabelais' easy
    chair,
Or praise the court or magnify mankind,
Or his grieved country's copper chains
    unbind.

The comparison is more kindly than just.
Swift was not an English Rabelais. He
rarely laughed ; he never shook in an

36

easy chair. He was as remote from the rollicking humour of Rabelais as he was from the light fingered cynicism of Voltaire, who by the way was too much a Frenchman of the 18th century thoroughly to appreciate his brother in irony. Rabelais lived laughing, and died laughing, and when he laughed the laughter of scorn, he would still be merry. Even Coleridge's witty phrase for Swift, "the soul of Rabelais, habitans in sicco," is less luminous than it seems. For, as I have said, the master-passion of Swift is anger against injustice and oppression. As he seldom laughs, so he is seldom the cause of laughter in others. Rather he is one who, having no illusions himself, would strip away the illusions which mask the faces of men. You marvel at the genius of *A Tale of a Tub* ; you do not laugh at it.

Moreover, there is a certain dryness in Swift's style, in the perfection of his work, in the essential justice of his opinions, a dryness in which the soul of Rabelais could never dwell. The humour of Rabelais is wide and spacious as the universe ; the wit of Swift is confined within the bounds of precision, and has no margin over. When in *Gulliver* he increases or diminishes the scale of life, that he may represent the small follies of his countrymen or picture their grosser, larger vices, he does it with a sort of mathematical accuracy which is wholly alien to the careless genius of Rabelais. In brief, the Frenchman and the Englishman fulfilled themselves, each in keeping with his own temper. They stand upon equal pinnacles of fame, and no good can come of their inapposite comparison.

The mathematical accuracy, with which in *Gulliver* Swift takes the measure of mankind, is allied to another faculty, which he shares with none other except Defoe. And that is the faculty of authentic and plausible narrative. By a hundred small touches, accurately designed, he renders the story of Gulliver's travels credible to its readers. Neither the dwarfs nor the giants make too great a demand upon our faith. And thus Swift achieves, in the face of far greater difficulties, the difficulties of the supernatural, the same sort of triumph of reality which Defoe achieved in *Robinson Crusoe*. No sooner were the *Travels* published than they were discussed gravely as a record of actual happenings. An Irish bishop, taking the view that was expected of him, said that the book was full of improbable lies, and that for his part he hardly believed a word of it. But it was Arbuthnot who sent to Swift the best news of his *Travels*. He prophesied truly for the book as great a run as John Bunyan, and he gave gratifying examples of its literal acceptance. "Lord Scarborough," he wrote, "who is no inventor of stories, told me that he fell in company with a master of a ship, who told him that he was very well acquainted with Gulliver, but that the printer had been mistaken, that he lived in Wapping, not in Rotherhithe. I lent the book to an old gentleman who went immediately to his map to search for Lilliput." The simplicity of the Irish bishop, the master of the ship, and the old gentleman, proved to Swift that he had not failed in the art of verisimilitude, and explains for us why *Gulliver* after two centuries is still the delight of children.

39

But Swift's highest gift of all was his gift of prose. It is this gift which has kept alive and fresh his political controversy, the kind of writing which is soonest withered by the blight of time. It is this gift which has ensured a lasting interest for every line which the Dean of St Patrick's touched with his pen. He could write well about a broomstick, it was said with perfect truth; and assuredly he never wrote ill about anything. We care nothing to-day about Wood's ha'pence or the restrictions put upon Irish manufactures, except that they gave an excuse for the solid eloquence of Swift. What then was the secret of his style? He has defined it himself: "Proper words in proper places," he tells a young clergyman, "make the true definition of style." He warns his fellows solemnly against the frequency of flat unnecessary epithets, and the folly of using old threadbare phrases. He cited it as an eminent virtue in the Brobdingnagians that they avoided nothing more than multiplying unnecessary words, or using various expressions. And it is

Dr Johnson, who, in his own despite, has most clearly defined the virtue of Swift's simplicity. Now, Dr Johnson did not like Swift, and a passage in Boswell's *Life*, dispraising *The Conduct of the Allies*, is an excellent comment upon the styles of the two great writers. Thus runs the passage: "*Johnson*. 'Sir, his *Conduct of the Allies* is a performance of very little ability.' 'Surely, Sir,' said Dr Douglas, 'you must allow it has strong facts.' *Johnson*. 'Why yes, Sir; but what is that to the merit of the composition? In the Sessions-paper of the Old Bailey there are strong facts. Housebreaking is a strong fact; robbery is a strong fact; and murder is a *mighty* strong fact; but is great praise due to the historian of these strong facts? No, Sir, Swift has told what he had to tell distinctly enough, but that is all. He had to count ten, and he has counted it right....Why, Sir, Tom Davies might have written *The Conduct of the Allies*.'"

Of course Johnson knew better than any other that Tom Davies could not have written *The Conduct of the Allies*. Indeed, had Tom Davies written it, no passion of its readers could have supplied its efficacy. But Johnson was convinced that the "wonder-working pamphlet" operated "by the mere weight of facts, with very little assistance from the hand that produced them." It is a strange opinion, held dialectically and perhaps perversely. The strength of facts and the strength of their expression have little enough to do with one another. In flaccid hands that "mighty strong fact," murder, might appear like a simple story for the tea-table. And Johnson, in pretending that Swift's effects depended less upon himself than upon his matter, was, I think, contrasting Swift's style with his own. Johnson sought in a sentence a balance and an arrangement, which all eyes might see, which all ears might hear. He was unhappy if there was not, here and there, a polysyllable to hold the lesser words in subjection. And thus he fashioned for himself that highly elaborated instrument, with which he hammered his thought into others. In the writings of Swift, no doubt, he missed the balance and the arrangement which were for him synonymous with style. And so, for the sake of argument, he was ready to assert that Tom Davies might have written *The Conduct of the Allies*.

Johnson, in thus criticizing Swift, reveals what was the aim of his own style, and by its opposite enlightens us about Swift's. The truth is that Swift's method of writing was at once more subtle and more just, if less nobly decorated, than Johnson's. That is to say, he was all for structure and not for ornament. Logic of thought, economy of phrase—these are the guiding principles of his prose. It is his great merit to have given a new force to the common forms of speech, to have set his words in so precise an order that the stress always falls where the sense demands it. His prose is not sonorous, save in pages; it is frequently inaccurate, as any pedant may see for himself. He depends not at all for his effect upon a curious vocabulary. He is as remote from the flamboyancy of his Elizabethan ancestors as from the prim elegance of Addison. So his style is inevitably clear, direct and appropriate. There is, so to say, the briefest interval between his thought and its expression ; and since his thought was commonly wit, it follows that the expression was witty also. Within the limits which he imposed on himself he could do what he liked with words. With greater ease than other men have attained he bent the stubborn English sentence to his will. He forged of English prose an instrument, which was apt for every enterprise : narrative and controversy were treated by him with equal happiness. The same hand, which lashed the follies and injustices of men, enlivened the loyal solitude of Stella with the incomparable journal. The same hand, which in the *Polite Conversation* gave us a perfect exposition of the commonplace, and invented a set of personages not one of which might boast a shred of character, penned also the savage satire of the *Directions to Servants*. Any one of these achievements is sufficient for an enduring fame, and with their sum Swift shall defy death, so long as English prose is read and understood.

In conclusion : Jonathan Swift may be

viewed from many points, and in many aspects. There are still those, who, with something of the eavesdropper's impertinence, would pierce the mystery of his loves. Others there are who would dwell willingly upon the tragic years in which he died slowly, like a tree from the top, and which seem to belong less to history than to medical science. But for those who care for humane letters the supreme interest and merit of Swift will always lie in the assured mastery wherewith he illustrates, as very few have ever illustrated them, the greatness and simplicity of our English tongue.

www.ingramcontent.com/pod-product-compliance
Ingram Content Group UK Ltd.
Pitfield, Milton Keynes, MK11 3LW, UK
UKHW042149280225
455719UK00001B/212